WORK-LIFE IN BALANCE

15 STRATEGIES TO CREATE A WORK-LIFE BALANCE YOU DESERVE

I0521512

Alison Begor

Alison Begor
Lexington, KY

Work-Life in Balance: 15 Strategies To Create a Work-Life Balance You Deserve / Alison Begor —1st ed.
ISBN 979-8-9852894-0-4

Table of Contents

This book is dedicated to my kids who fill me with joy (and endless amounts of soccer cleats).

*"I've learned that you can't have everything and
do everything at the same time."*

Oprah Winfrey

My Story

I had one of those days when I knew I wasn't
managing my stress level very well, and I felt one
step away from panic. I felt overwhelmed, and my
work-life balance was completely out of whack.

My corporate job was hectic, and it was the last
two weeks of summer break for my 2 kids. I was
dealing with several work deadlines, attending
multiple meetings per day, while also managing my
kids' back-to-school shopping, appointments, and
school open houses. As part of getting ready for
school, my kids received haircuts that they hated,
which was, of course, all my fault. They both were
in need of new school clothes, and I wasn't even

sure when we could fit clothes shopping into our schedule.

Added to all that, I felt the pressure of making sure we had a fun summer, but we had barely crossed anything off our summer bucket list. I now had two weeks to make sure we had a summer's-worth of fun. In addition, my son started playing high school soccer, and even though I had been a soccer mom for years, navigating eight practices a week for high school called for a new level of organization.

Finally, that stress-filled day wouldn't be complete unless there was something wrong on the housing front. That week, I also heard a dripping sound coming from inside my wall that freaked me out. Luckily, the plumber confirmed everything was okay; however, I had to make time for him to check everything out and, as a result, had a hole in my hallway ceiling that I needed to fix.

And so on, and so on, and so on...

I wasn't managing my work-life balance very well at all that day and knew I needed to go back to my strategies that we will cover in this book to help lessen the overwhelm and bring a greater sense of calm. In the past, I would have accepted that this was life and that I would always be overwhelmed. Maybe you have felt that way too?

Now, with the help of these 15 strategies I am going to share with you, I can better manage my stress, recognize that life will get hairy, and create a work-life that feels aligned and that I love. I hope that you can find several strategies here that will improve your work-life balance too!

How do you define work-life balance?

When you search for work-life balance on Google, you will see almost as many results for why work-life balance is a myth as there are results on how to improve your work-life balance. Do you feel like having work-life balance is a myth? For years, I thought it was a myth, yet that didn't stop me from always searching out ways to improve my work-life balance.

The Cambridge Dictionary defines work-life balance as "the amount of time you spend doing your job compared with the amount of time you spend with your family and doing things you enjoy." One interpretation of this definition is that you should be spending the SAME amount of time on work and life in any given week or on any given day.

With this definition, you can imagine perfectly balanced scales. For anyone who has tried measuring just the right amount of anything at the grocery store, it can take several tries before the weight is balanced. Striving to achieve a life where everything we do is perfectly balanced in equal amounts is not only unrealistic but unattainable. No wonder work-life balance can feel so hard and feel like a myth!

I choose to define work-life balance as a state of flow and alignment. I view the balance as circular and I describe it as feeling balance within my own body. I visualize balance looking like the ocean. Sometimes the tide is high, and sometimes it is low. There can be high waves or there can be calm waters. Even with the different changes in the ocean, the ocean water is always moving and flowing. For me, that means at times, work is going to receive more of my time and at other times, my life is going to receive more of my time. The key is finding a flow to my work-life that feels aligned for me, meets my goals and matches the feelings I desire and want for my life.

Merriam-Webster has nine different definitions for the word balance. One definition is "stability produced by an even distribution of weight" which is the definition we are trying to move away from when it comes to our work-life. (Again, imagine the perfectly balanced scales.)

A definition I love is "mental and emotional steadiness." Isn't that what we are trying to achieve when we want better work-life balance? A state of mental and emotional steadiness?

As you think about what work-life balance means to you, think about the feelings you would have with an ideal work-life balance. Many of my clients want feelings of calm, peace, relief, and spaciousness. For me, my core feelings are peace, calm, and joy. When I feel my life is out of alignment now, I can make adjustments so that I end my day feeling calm. Once you know the feelings you want to achieve, it's easier to figure out what adjustments you want to make to achieve those feelings to have a better sense of flow and to create a work-life balance you desire and deserve.

How to use this book

This book contains 15 strategies that can be used to help improve your work-life balance. You do not need to do everything in this book to see improvements. In fact, I recommend starting with ONE thing to change or implement in your life. As you start to incorporate the strategy into your life and you feel ready, you can choose the next strategy to implement.

You may want to read the book cover to cover before choosing the strategy that works best for you as a starting place. You may decide to jump straight to the strategy that interests you the most and to block everything out for now. There isn't a perfect way to use this book. The best way to read and use this book is the one that works for you.

It's designed to be picked up as needed. Consider it a reference and guide as you are making changes to improve your work life balance

Are you not sure what strategy to choose to implement first? Feeling overwhelmed by the choices? Start with the strategy that feels easiest to you. Even making one small change in a few minutes per day will add up to hours saved and better work-life balance.

TIME
MANAGEMENT

"Either you run the day, or the day runs you."

Jim Rohn

Maintain Work Hours

Many people are overworked either by working long hours or being tied to their emails even while not at work. Does that sound like you?

Working longer hours does not lead to higher productivity in fact it can have a negative effect. Research[1] has shown that overwork can lead to a host of health problems that aren't good for you or your employer. Working too many hours can lead to impaired sleep, impaired memory, depression, heart conditions, and more. Overworked employees are bad for employers as well because these employees have higher absenteeism rates, more turnover, and increased health insurance costs.

In addition, working long hours can lead to lower productivity and increased stress, as you may feel that work is taking over your life, which definitely isn't good for you or your work-life balance.

Setting work hours (and keeping them) is one strategy to help regain time in your schedule and regain balance. I believe that work fills the time that you give it, so try giving your work less time.

You may believe that you won't be able to accomplish as much working fewer hours. Have you ever gone on vacation and felt the rush of energy and productivity before you go? It can often feel like you accomplish more in the week before leaving for vacation than you do in a whole month.

Use your vacation energy and commit to keeping to your work end time for one week, and see if you notice a difference in how you feel. Plan your work to fit the time you give it, and use your extra time to do something that you enjoy.

Question to Ponder

What are your ideal work hours?

_____

_____

_____

_____

Action Step

I will commit to the following work hours this week:

_____

_____

_____

_____

"We think, mistakenly, that success is the result of the amount of time we put in at work, instead of the quality of time we put in."

Arianna Huffington

Time of Day

For years, I have heard that the most productive people are up early in the morning. I believed that the only way to succeed was to wake up at 5:00 a.m., exercise, and accomplish all my important work before noon. I used to beat myself up because I struggled to be a morning person however my brain doesn't do its best thinking in the morning. How was I ever going to be successful? I didn't fit the morning person mold. I fit the don't-talk-to-me-before-my-coffee mold.

Through trial and error, I discovered two important things:

1. It's okay if your most productive time is later in the day. You can still be successful.

2. Just because you are not a self-described "morning person", you can still have effective morning routines.

What I learned about my productivity is that I am most productive around midday and in the evening. So for me, that is from 10 a.m. to 2 p.m. and usually about 7 p.m. to 9 p.m. Knowing this about myself allows me to schedule my time in a way that works for my optimum productivity. I schedule my most important tasks during my most productive time. I schedule meetings and other administrative tasks during the other hours of the day. This allows me to focus my highest energy on the largest projects on my plate.

In addition, I implemented a better morning routine. The old me would hit snooze multiple times, hurry through my shower, rush to get everyone out the door and start drinking coffee once I arrived at work.

Now, I don't use the snooze button anymore. If you had told me that was possible, I wouldn't have believed you... just ask my college roommate! I spend time in the morning meditating, planning the day, and enjoying coffee. Coffee is a huge pleasure of mine, and taking the time to really enjoy the first cup of the day sets my day off on a great foot.

When is your most productive time of the day? Are you a morning person, a night owl, or something in between? If you don't know your most productive time of day. Track your tasks and energy for three days. As you are tracking, make notes of your feelings. At the end of three days, look for patterns in your schedule for when you felt most energized, when you accomplished the most work and/or when you felt the best.

After you have figured out your most productive time of the day, take a look at your schedule and see if your tasks and appointments line up with your natural energy. The more you are able to match your energy, the more your productivity will increase, and the better you will feel.

Questions to Ponder

When is your best time of day?

_____

_____

_____

_____

How can you use your energy to better serve you?

_____

_____

_____

_____

_____

Action Step

I am making the changes below to better match my
tasks to my most productive time(s) of day:

_____

_____

_____

_____

_____

_____

_____

_____

_____

_____

_____

"The brain cannot multitask. Multitasking, when it comes to paying attention, is a myth."

John Medina

Stop Multitasking

Several years ago, being able to multitask was all the buzz in business. During interviews, candidates often stated that their strength was being good at multitasking. People who were good multitaskers were seen as productive and great workers.

What if I told you that no one is actually multitasking at all? And if the premise of multitasking actually takes more time and reduces productivity?

Multitasking is believed to be when you are able to do two things at once; however, what really happens during multitasking is the brain makes quick switches back and forth between the two tasks. Your brain is constantly starting and stopping on each task which is known in psychology as serial tasking not multitasking.

Research from the American Psychological Association[2] shows that multitasking is inefficient and not productive. Your brain takes time to switch back and forth to each task. All of the transition time adds up and leads to more lost time throughout the day. Some of the research has shown that multitasking can actually take up to 40 percent more time than focusing on one task at a time.

So what can you do, especially when you have so many competing priorities in one day?

First, schedule your day to focus on one task at a time. Choose your most important tasks (hopefully in your zone of genius[3]) to do during your most productive time of the day.

Next, limit distractions. Completely eliminating distractions is not realistic for anyone however limiting distractions will have a big impact on your ability to focus on one task at a time. Some ideas for limiting distractions include turning off your email notifications or shutting down your email program, putting your phone on "do not disturb," and marking the time on your calendar as a meeting with yourself.

Finally, take breaks. Taking breaks is a good way for your brain to focus on other tasks and on the items that could be a distraction for you, allowing you to focus more intently during your work time.

This week, set a small goal to improve your focus on one task at a time. Not sure what to choose? Decide to set designated times to check your email, every three hours for example. At the designated times, open, read and respond to all emails. When the time is up, close your email program and resume your work. Before you know it, you will be a single-focused task pro!

Questions to Ponder

Notice where you are multitasking, how do you feel?

_____

_____

_____

_____

How can you schedule your time to focus on one task at a time?

_____

_____

_____

_____

_____

Action Step

I will commit to the following schedule change to focus on one task at a time this week:

_____

_____

_____

_____

_____

_____

_____

_____

_____

_____

_____

"The key is not spending time, but in investing it."

Stephen R. Covey

Time Blocks

Have you ever had a day when you were busy doing a million things, yet didn't cross anything off of your to-do list? Or maybe you were too busy doing time-sucking administrative tasks. Your larger projects didn't receive the time they deserve, and therefore they didn't get done?

As we learned in the last strategy, stop multitasking, it takes time for your brain to switch between tasks. Constantly switching tasks can take up to 40% of your productive time. Instead of multitasking, try time blocking.

Using time blocking is one strategy that can have an immediate impact on having more time in your schedule and accomplishing more on your to-do list.

I use time blocking in two different ways: batching similar tasks and matching tasks to my energy.

The first part of the time block strategy is to batch similar tasks. You may have heard of batching before and the idea is to do similar tasks in one block of time, which will help to reduce the amount of time that your brain takes to switch between different types of tasks. In addition, depending on the task, you are only preparing for the task one time before the time block instead of multiple times that week or that day.

For example, if you record podcasts or videos, you may choose to batch your recording all in one time block or on one day. Another task that everyone can batch is reading and responding to email. How often are you distracted by email notifications? Do you stop what you are doing to read and respond to email multiple times per day? By time-blocking email and committing to opening your email at designated times per day, you can reduce notification distraction and reduce the total time spent on email.

Other ideas for tasks you may batch include expense reports, billing and invoicing, preparing for classes or presentations, writing, and administrative paperwork.

The second part of the time block strategy is to match the tasks with your best time of day. For most people, energy naturally goes up and down throughout the day. As we learned in the time-of-day strategy, matching tasks and meetings to our natural energy flow is a great way not only to be more productive but also to save time in our schedules each day.

Utilizing time blocks through batching tasks and matching your energy will help you save time each week. Try it for one week and see how much time you have freed up in your schedule. Even if it's only 10 minutes per day, that adds up to 50 minutes in a work week. Notice how you feel and how you can spend those extra minutes on something that feels good to you or gives you more space in your schedule to breathe.

Question to Ponder

What tasks can you batch and time block?

_____

_____

_____

_____

Action Step

I will batch and time block these tasks this week:

_____

_____

_____

_____

CARE FOR SELF

STRATEGY FIVE

*"We need to do a better job of putting ourselves higher on
our own 'to do' list."*

Michelle Obama

Prioritize Yourself

You need to prioritize yourself. Yes, you.

This strategy is probably the hardest to hear, and
one of the hardest to implement. Many of us,
especially women, are great at helping others. We
pride ourselves on the care and concern we give to
our family, friends, neighbors, and colleagues, but
it's often at the expense of ourselves.

We may wonder why others don't seem to
prioritize and help us in the same way that we help
them and it's probably because we haven't
prioritized ourselves first.

Last year, one of my son's soccer practices was
changed after we arrived at the facility and about
five minutes before practice was scheduled to start.

We suddenly received a message that there had been a schedule mix-up at the facility and practice was being pushed back by an hour.

I understand that schedules change, things come up and sometimes stuff just happens. We waited for about 10 minutes to see what the coach would decide to do before I made the decision to prioritize myself. I told my son that my schedule was important too and that we weren't able to wait another hour in the parking lot for practice to start. I jokingly told him #parentsschedulesmatter (which isn't wrong).

I'm glad I listened to my gut, prioritized myself and my schedule that day and left. About 10 minutes after we left, the coach sent a message that practice was cancelled because of the mix-up. I didn't feel that I had wasted more time and I didn't feel resentful.

My son's soccer practice is one example of how I prioritized myself by taking my own needs and schedule into account rather than always accommodating my kids' schedules. You are likely faced with many decisions during the day through which you can choose to prioritize yourself or choose to prioritize others.

Just as we are told when flying to put on our own oxygen mask before helping others, we must do that in our daily decisions. Prioritizing ourselves before helping others helps us give from a better energy. We can't pour into others if our own cup is empty.

Question to Ponder

Where do you currently prioritize yourself?

_____

_____

_____

_____

Action Step

I will prioritize myself in these ways this week:

_____

_____

_____

_____

STRATEGY SIX

"Amazing things happen when you're having fun and doing something you love."

Jenna Lyons

Do Things You Love

Several years ago I attended a great professional development session about using my own authentic voice instead of being a cover band (or always doing the same things as others.) I was excited to attend as I knew the presenter always delivered great material and I was attending with friends.

At one point in the presentation, she asked us to name some of the things that we love doing. One by one my fellow attendees raised their hands and said things like:

"I love playing the violin. Playing in the community orchestra really fills me up."

"Animals. Spending time with my dogs at the end of a long day brings me so much joy."

"I love running! I find inner peace and time to think when I run."

I prayed she wouldn't call on me. I had no idea what I loved to do, let alone what would bring me joy. I was stuck.

Over the course of the next few years, I began to observe what I enjoyed doing. I thought back to what I loved to do as a child and as a younger adult. I began to try different activities again to find the ones that filled me with joy.

I also had to schedule time on my calendar to do the things that I loved. It was challenging to recognize that I needed time for me, more than just being alone while in the shower.

Over time, I started scheduling more time for what I love and figuring out what I love to do. I love flower arranging and almost always have arrangements of fresh flowers in my home. I love to read and always have stacks of books on my nightstand. I love to spend time outdoors and my son and we rediscovered our love for hiking together.

It can still be a challenge to find the time, however by doing things I love that fill me up on a daily basis, I feel more at peace, more able to deal with daily stress, and more able to find balance in my life.

Questions to Ponder

What activities and/or hobbies do you love to do?

_____

_____

_____

_____

What activities and/or hobbies would you like to try?

_____

_____

_____

_____

Action Step

I will commit to doing this one activity that I love
this week:

_____

_____

_____

_____

_____

_____

_____

_____

_____

_____

"Self-care doesn't necessarily mean jogging!"

Sandra Oh

Self-Care

What comes to mind when you hear the words "self-care"?

Maybe you thought of taking bubble baths, massages, going for a walk, or having a spa day.

Those are all great ways to practice self-care and yet there is so much more to self-care. The definition of self-care is "the practice of taking an active role in protecting one's own well-being and happiness."

A few years ago, I didn't think that I had time for self-care. I would laugh at the suggestions of putting myself first on my calendar. I didn't think it was possible because I had so many responsibilities as a working mom. After working all day, managing the household and parenting my kids, there literally was not time for anything else, especially not for self-care. Maybe you can relate?

I worked with a coach who challenged me to keep a self-care journal for two weeks. Even though I knew I didn't have time for self-care, keeping the journal and seeing the results of my lack of self-care were astonishing.

I kept up with the journal and began actively finding ways to incorporate self-care into my day. For me, it looked like:

- Listening to a podcast while walking my dog
- Sitting outside for 15 minutes to read
- Setting a boundary and honoring that boundary
- Saying no to things I don't want to do
- Spending more time connecting with friends
- Drinking my first cup of coffee out on the patio

After two months of keeping a self-care journal and increasing the amount of time I spent on self-care, I noticed that I:

- Had more energy
- Created more time in my day, not less

- Had more patience for my kids
- Felt happier overall

Making time for self-care helps us have more time, even though this process sounds counterintuitive. It really does work for us to put on our own oxygen masks first before helping others.

Self-care doesn't have to be only about bubble baths (although they are lovely.) Self-care can be honoring your boundaries, honoring your "no" and honoring yourself.

40 Self-Care ideas

1. Say No
2. Take a Bubble Bath
3. Go on a Nature Walk
4. Enjoy a Phone Call with a Friend
5. Rest
6. Read a Book
7. Listen to a Podcast
8. Knit
9. Choose not to Argue
10. Drink a Cup of Tea
11. Arrange Flowers
12. Take a Spa Day
13. Spend Time with Pets
14. Practice Yoga
15. Ride a Bike
16. Use Positive Self-Talk
17. Use Perfume/Cologne
18. Light a Candle
19. Sleep on Soft Sheets
20. Sit Outside

21. Dance in the Rain

22. Buy Yourself Flowers

23. Order Dinner In

24. Watch Funny Cat Videos

25. Dance to Your Favorite Song

26. Sing in the Shower

27. Go for a Drive

28. Enforce Your Boundaries

29. Stretch

30. Declutter

31. Watch the Sunrise/Sunset

32. Garden

33. Wear Your Favorite Outfit

34. Drink Water

35. Go on a Date

36. Take a Day Off

37. Nap

38. Meditate

39. Color

40. Shut Down Social Media

Question to Ponder

What are some additional self-care activities that you enjoy?

_____

_____

_____

_____

Action Step

I will commit to doing this one self-care activity today:

_____

_____

_____

_____

"Wherever you are, be there totally."

Eckhart Tolle

Manage Your Mind

I am very hard on myself and I used to be the queen of negative self-talk. Maybe you can relate? I thought I needed to do everything and do it at an A+ level. If I did anything less, the negative self-talk would start roaring in my brain.

Some days, the stress would be so high that my mind felt as if it were on overdrive with my thoughts going down a million different highways. I used to have thoughts that I believed when in fact my brain was lying to me.

Some of those thoughts included:

- "There is no way out. All working moms live unbalanced lives."

- "Everyone is busy. Who am I to complain?"

- "If I only planned my meals better on the weekend, my life wouldn't feel as stressful."

- "I lack discipline because I can't seem to get it together enough to stop ordering dinner out three nights a week."

- "Work is supposed to be hard. Just deal with it."

Through working with a therapist and a coach, I began to learn how to better manage and redirect my thoughts. More importantly, I learned that most of my thoughts were lies.

Some tools you can use to work on managing your mind include meditation, mindfulness, and thought work. Working with a coach is a great way to learn how to redirect your thoughts so that you feel better.

Meditation has been used for thousands of years and is the practice of developing intentional focus. You can practice meditation quietly on your own, with the assistance of an app, such as Headspace or Calm, or even with walking meditations. Meditating only a couple of minutes a day can positively impact your overall health with possible results of increased focus, decreased stress, and better sleep.

The practice of mindfulness has gained popularity in recent years and calls us to bring attention to what we are currently doing. How often do you walk into a room and forget why you went in there? (Umm, for me, more often than I care to admit!) Practicing mindfulness helps us to stay in the present moment without judgment.

You can try it now. Find something in the room to observe in a new way. Pay attention to what you see, the color, texture, and shape. Notice if you see anything different about the object you choose. Observe and note any new awareness. Mindfulness can be done anywhere and at any time. Practice mindfulness throughout your day to be fully present in everything you do.

Thought work is the practice of noticing negative thoughts and consciously changing those thoughts. Many coaches utilize thought work in their practice. I really like Byron Katie's[4] "The Work" which focuses on four questions:

1. Is it true?
2. Can you absolutely know that it's true?
3. How do you react, what happens, when you believe that thought?
4. Who would you be without that thought?

Using the material on her website, you can go into more depth and practice doing "The Work" including the four questions listed above and thought turnarounds. I highly recommend trying it and seeing what thoughts you can turn around. One thing to note is that thought work is definitely a practice. Many of our thoughts have been in our brains for a very long time and have dug very deep trenches. By continuing to practice, we can create new pathways and pull ourselves out from the negative trenches.

Bringing attention to our thoughts and managing our minds is a great strategy to create the work-life balance that we desire.

Questions to Ponder

What are some ways you currently manage your mind?

_____

_____

_____

_____

What new ways would you like to try?

_____

_____

_____

_____

Action Step

I will commit to taking the first step in this one way to manage my mind this week:

_____

_____

_____

_____

_____

_____

_____

_____

_____

_____

_____

MAKE & SAVE TIME

"You don't have to make yourself miserable to be successful."

Andrew Wilkinson

Take Breaks

Time management and productivity are very popular topics in today's business world. People are always looking for ways to do more with less as well as increase productivity in the limited hours they do have. Schedules are busy and employees are often pulled in many directions. So what is the number one strategy to increase productivity and have a better work-life balance? Take more breaks.

Have you heard of people who do their best thinking in the shower? (Maybe that's you?) Thinking in the shower is a good example of how breaks can help the mind. Taking regular breaks throughout the day has many benefits.

By taking regular breaks, we can prevent decision fatigue. Coming back to problems fresh allows us to make good, clear decisions. Making multiple decisions in a row without breaks can cause us to make the easiest decision, which is not always the right decision and can lead to memory impairment and decision fatigue.

Stretching, moving, or taking a walk is a great way to take a break. Regular physical movement helps not only our physical health but also our mental health.

Often, when we're working on a difficult problem, taking a walking break can help stimulate our creative juices and help us think of new solutions and ideas.

Just as sleep helps our brains with learning and memory formation, resting while awake can also have the same benefits. Ferris Jabr states the following in a *Scientific American*[5] article: "Downtime replenishes the brain's stores of attention and motivation, encourages productivity and creativity, and is essential to both achieve our highest levels of performance and simply form stable memories in everyday life…Moments of respite may even be necessary to keep one's moral compass in working order and maintain a sense of self."

Taking breaks and resting during the day, even if just for 5 to10 minutes, helps increase our productivity levels.

Good breaks are done away from devices. Some ideas for a break include going for a walk, stretching, drinking a cup of coffee (or tea), taking lunch, practicing 15 minutes of self-care, catching up with a colleague, or daydreaming. When is it not a good time to take a break? When you are in the flow. When you are in the flow and rhythm of your work, it's best to keep working and take a break at a natural stopping point.

Now you have a great reason to take a walk for that cup of coffee during the work day – it will increase your productivity and improve your work-life balance.

Questions to Ponder

How am I currently taking breaks?

_____

_____

_____

Where can I take more breaks during the day?

_____

_____

_____

How will I spend my break?

_____

_____

Action Step

I will commit to taking breaks at the following times this week and here are some ways I will spend my breaks:

_____

_____

_____

_____

_____

_____

_____

_____

_____

_____

"Never get so busy making a living that you forget to make a life."

Dolly Parton

Take Real Time Off

Do you take regular vacation days? When you are on vacation, do you REALLY take that time off meaning you have unplugged from work (you don't even check email)? If so, fabulous! If not, now is a great time to plan REAL time off.

Did you know that employees who take vacation time are more productive? In the book, *The Happiness Advantage*[6], Shawn Achor shares that "the brain can think positively, productivity improves by 31 percent, sales increase by 37 percent, and creativity and revenues can triple" when employees take time off.

Did you also know that a study reported in the *Harvard Business Review*[7] found that employees who took off fewer than 10 days per year had a 34.6

percent chance of receiving a raise or bonus and employees who took more than 10 days off per year had a 65.4 percent chance of receiving a raise or bonus? If taking real time off increases my chance of receiving more money, that's a no brainer for me.

Being able to step away from work to focus on other priorities in life, including relaxing, helps to rejuvenate your mind and body. In order to fully feel the effects, you do need to take the time off. No checking work email while you are away. Not being in constant communication with the office can be difficult, but setting expectations and boundaries in advance of a vacation will help you to stay away from your email account. In addition, if you lead an organization or a team, the example you set will help all your employees be able to fully reap the benefits of their time away from the office.

You do not always have to go somewhere to take your vacation leave. Staycations to explore the place where you live are great ways to use time off and take a break.

Taking real time off will help you disconnect from work, rejuvenate, spend time with people you love, and doing things you love will help you feel more engaged when you are back at work.

Questions to Ponder

How am I currently taking real time off?

_____

_____

_____

What change(s) can I make during my time off?

_____

_____

_____

How does that make me feel?

_____

_____

Action Step

I will schedule the following real time off in the next 90 days:

_____

_____

_____

_____

_____

_____

_____

_____

_____

_____

STRATEGY ELEVEN

"It's really clear that the most precious resource we all have is time."

Steve Jobs

Find Shortcuts

I love shortcuts.

Years ago, I used to spend my time cutting coupons only to then spend time organizing them, usually forgetting to bring them to the store, and throwing them away when they expired. I realized after a while that the time I spent doing this activity cost me way more than the money I was saving in coupons. At that point, I realized my time has value. To create a life I don't want to retire from, I needed to value my time, so I began focusing on finding shortcuts.

Some of my favorite shortcuts are mobile ordering and grocery delivery.

A few years ago, my sons wanted to check out the mania of Thanksgiving night Black Friday shopping. We went to Target and my sons' eyes were wide as they saw the line that snaked around the store with no end in sight. There were only a couple of items we were interested in purchasing so I pulled out my phone and placed my order. We did this for one other store as well. The next morning, I drove up, picked up my orders and was done in 15 minutes. Time saved with a shortcut.

What shortcuts do you utilize to make your life easier?

Shortcut and Timesaver Ideas
1. Mobile Order
2. Place a Grocery Delivery (Instacart, Whole Foods, etc)
3. Curbside Pickup Your Shopping
4. Order Meal boxes (Hello Fresh, Home Chef, Blue Apron, etc.)
5. Hire a Personal Chef
6. Use Mobile Banking
7. Use Paper Plates
8. Hire a House cleaner
9. Turn Off Phone Notifications
10. Make Decisions
11. Use Email Templates and Canned Responses

Questions to Ponder

What other shortcut ideas do you have?

_____

_____

_____

_____

How do you already use shortcuts to simplify your life?

_____

_____

_____

_____

Action Step

I will try implementing the following shortcuts:

_____

_____

_____

_____

_____

_____

_____

_____

_____

_____

_____

SAY YES TO YOU

"Balance is not better time management, but better boundary management. Balance means making choices and enjoying those choices."

Betsy Jacobson

Boundaries

Several years ago, when my son was around 2, I was transitioning between jobs. It was my last week at my current job, and I was spending one day at the new job to start transitioning. I had been there for about three hours when my phone rang. I saw that it was my son's daycare and instantly felt a pit in my stomach. Rarely did they call during the work day with good news, usually it was a report of how my child threw up and I needed to leave work immediately to come and pick him up.

I answered the phone and it was worse than I thought. My son had banged his lip on a wood slide and the director was fairly certain he would need stitches. I quickly explained to my new boss that I needed to leave (they were very understanding), and I picked up my son to take him to the ER. His dad met us there.

While we were in the ER waiting to find out the best way to stitch up my son's lip, my phone rang again. It was the job I was leaving in a week. I answered the call. I thought if I explained that I was in the ER with my son, my co-worker would understand and hang up. Instead, without missing a beat, they proceeded to ask their work question. It involved a multi-part answer, however, it wasn't urgent and could have easily waited until the next day. My attention was split, and I felt more frazzled.

I knew then that I needed better boundaries. I shouldn't have answered the phone. That was on me. I was with my family, in an emergency, on my day off, and work wasn't important at that time.

I began practicing better work boundaries and discovering the many types of boundaries I could have that would ultimately prioritize me and save me time.

My ability to set boundaries was tested in March 2020 at the beginning of the global pandemic. Working from home beginning in mid-March was a sudden change. Previously, I had always gone to the office for work and used my home office sparingly. Even though I had some flexibility in my job, I still arrived at the office at the same time each morning, had my office routine, and headed home in the evening. I used my commute to create a boundary between work and home.

After a couple of weeks of working from home, I began to realize that this change was more permanent than the temporary two weeks first predicted to flatten the curve. I set up my home office to be more conducive to a full day's work while also setting up my children for virtual school. Boundaries became even more important as work and school were both happening from home… not to mention that my home office was in a corner of my bedroom, which was less than ideal.

Now was the time to figure out what boundaries I needed both to manage expectations, communication and performance at work, as well as to manage the space between work and family life at home.

Many of my clients also reported that everything changed for them in mid-March. The pandemic forced many into their homes, some with family, where work and home lives collided. They hadn't worked 100 percent from home before and felt that they needed to be tied to their devices to prove they were still working hard. Expectations increased, mostly pressure from within, to prove their value and be reachable all the time. Without having good boundaries, my clients patience wore thin, their focus on important projects decreased, and their tempers sometimes flared. Working during a crisis is hard. Working during a crisis without good boundaries is even harder.

Some of the boundaries that my clients implemented and utilized during the pandemic continue to be useful whenever you must set good work boundaries.

Do you believe that you need to be available 24/7 to respond immediately to emails to show you are committed to your work?
(You don't.)

You may have a boss or a work environment with this expectation but unless you have had a specific conversation about what working from home entails, your belief is only an
assumption.

To start having healthier boundaries, consider the steps below to begin creating and implementing your own boundaries.

Step 1: Decide on your basic work hours each day giving yourself some flexibility. You may decide that you are most productive and have the most quiet time early in the morning, scheduling a block of time from 5:30 am to 8:30 am. You should focus on your most important tasks during this period. Save responding to emails for later. As part of your work hours, decide what time you will start work

AND finish work each day. When you are done for the day, close your laptop and turn your notifications off. Communicate with your team on how to reach you in an emergency and trust that they will. Emails are not an emergency, and they can wait until tomorrow.

Step 2: Choose a Visual Cue. You may have a workspace that is close to your living and or sleeping space. You might choose a visual cue such as turning a lamp on or off helps your brain know when you are working and when you are spending time with your family, with yourself, and on leisure activities. Because my home office is in my bedroom, I use my desk lamp as my visual cue between work and home.

Step 3. Create a boundary with your schedule and inform your colleagues of your work schedule. It can be very easy for work colleagues to schedule meetings in all your calendar's blank space and before you know it, you have a day full of back-to-back meetings leaving little time for your own priorities and no time for balance. When you plan your work hours, block out time for your important tasks as well as your downtime. Figure out which times of the day work best for meetings. You are in control of your calendar. You can say no to meetings and suggest better times.

Creating clear boundaries between work and home is good not only for your mental health but also for your work productivity. Having healthy work boundaries will help you feel more in control of your work and experience more joy in your life.

Question to Ponder

What are some boundaries that I can implement?

_____

_____

_____

_____

Action Step

I will implement the following boundary this week:

_____

_____

_____

_____

"Striving for excellence motivates you; striving for perfection is demoralizing."

Harriet Braiker

Forget Perfection

I have a confession.

I am a recovering perfectionist. I was so deep in perfectionism that I didn't even THINK that I was a perfectionist.

When I first faced the thought that I was a perfectionist, I was adamant that there was no way it was true. I mean, my house was a mess and nowhere near the magazine look that I wanted to have. How could I possibly be a perfectionist if I felt like a mess?

And yet, it was true.

I was letting perfectionism stop me from trying to achieve the look and feel in my house that I wanted. I was letting perfectionism stop me from having the work-life balance I desired and DESERVED.

Maybe you can relate?

I have talked to many clients and friends who feel like they have to be perfect. Even writing this book, I had to fight the urge for it to be perfect as I knew that if I waited until it was perfect, the book would never be published.

Letting go of my perfectionism has been one of the hardest strategies for me yet it's also one of the most effective. Letting go of perfectionism has allowed me to have more time and more joy in my life.

Where have you been letting perfectionism stop you from living your life?

Questions to Ponder

What are areas in my work and life where I feel the need to be perfect?

_____

_____

_____

_____

How would it feel to let go of perfectionism?

_____

_____

What do I think will happen?

_____

_____

Action Step

I will let go of perfectionism in this one area this week:

_____

_____

_____

_____

_____

_____

_____

_____

_____

_____

_____

STRATEGY FOURTEEN

"No" is a complete sentence."

Anne Lamott

Say No

Many of us believed that we could have it all and in doing so also believed that we couldn't say no. We wanted to make sure we were doing all the right things as family members, while also saying yes to everything at work so that we were in the room, we were seen as an excellent team player, and we would be considered for a promotion.

Somehow along the way, being busy became a badge of honor. It's as though we all thought there would be a prize for who was busiest. Busy isn't a badge of honor. The only prize is exhaustion, overwhelm, and a life out of balance.

Saying yes all the time can lead to feelings of resentment. Maybe it's for the party you agreed to attend, and now you're thinking of an excuse to get out of it. Maybe it's for bringing homemade

Pinterest-worthy cupcakes to the school's winter party. The resentment grows as you are baking in the kitchen after a long day at work and kids' afterschool activities while everyone else in your house sleeps. It's even better when the first batch burns and you have to start all over again (ahem).

It's okay to say no. It might feel uncomfortable. And others may be surprised or upset when we say no (especially the first time).

Saying no is important.

Saying no to others is saying yes to ourselves.

Questions to Ponder

When have I said yes lately that resulted in feelings of resentment?

_____

_____

_____

Where can I say no?

_____

_____

_____

How would it feel to say no to others?

_____

_____

Action Step

I will practice saying no this week by:

_____

_____

_____

_____

_____

_____

_____

_____

_____

_____

_____

_____

STRATEGY FIFTEEN

"Always trying new things is always more fun, and it can be scary, but it's always more fun in the end."

John Krasinski

Try Something New

Not too long ago, I was feeling a bit bored by the routine of our lives. I had lots of reasons to be grateful however the monotony of work, school, homework, and sports had begun to make me feel stuck.

I decided in order to feel more alive again, I needed to try something new. I looked for events happening on the weekend and found a night hike happening at a local adventure place. Even better, the night hike was free, and the adventure place was only a15 minutes' drive from our home.

We arrived for the hike and the guide gave us headlamps. She told us a little about the hike however I still did not know what to expect. As we began our hike, I was concerned that it would be mostly hiking through fields and not very interesting. Once we approached a creek, I realized I was wrong.

Seeing the rock structures and creek with our headlamps was very cool. All of us had fun skipping stones in the creek. After we hiked a little farther, we climbed a bunch of rocks (much more strenuous that I was expecting) and arrived at another section of the creek. The guide checked the depth of the water and as a result the guide suggested taking off our shoes and rolling up our pants to cross.

Hiking across water, barefoot, at night, using only the light from our headlamps was definitely a new experience. I loved the hike and felt completely invigorated. Trying something new was exactly what I needed and my mood improved immediately.

Research[8] released in 2020 backs up what I experienced. They found that having new and different experiences is directly linked to increased happiness. They also found that positive feelings may cause people to seek out more new and diverse experiences.

In addition to taking breaks, practicing self-care, and doing things you love, trying something new is a great way to enhance your emotions and feel more balanced in your life.

Question to Ponder
What new activities would I like to try?

_____

_____

_____

_____

Action Step

I will try the following new activity this week:

_____

_____

_____

_____

NEXT STEPS

Choose one strategy to work on for the next two weeks. Journal how you feel at the beginning of the two week period and journal how you feel and the time saved at the end of the two week period. Share your win on social media and tag @alison.begor

Join the She Leads community at Facebook to continue the conversation at www.facebook.com/groups/sheleadsgroup

Visit alisonbegor.com for more free resources and to join my email list.

REFERENCES

1. Carmichael, Sarah Green. "The Research Is Clear: Long Hours Backfire for People and for Companies." August 19, 2015. https://hbr.org/2015/08/the-research-is-clear-long-hours-backfire-for-people-and-for-companies

2. American Psychological Association. "Multitasking: Switching costs." March 20, 2006. https://www.apa.org/research/action/multitask

3. Hendricks, Gay. *The Big Leap: Conquer Your Hidden Fear and Take Life to the Next Level.* New York: HarperOne, 2009

4. Byron, Katie. "The Work is a Practice." Accessed, October 1, 2021. https://thework.com/instruction-the-work-byron-katie/

5. Jabr, Ferris. "Why Your Brain Needs More Downtime." *Scientific American*, October, 15 2013. https://www.scientificamerican.com/article/mental-downtime/

6. Achor, Shawn. *The Happiness Advantage: The Seven Principles of Positive Psychology That Fuel Success and Performance at Work.* New York: Crown Business, 2010

7. Achor, Shawn and Gielan, Michelle. "The Data-Driven Case for Vacation." July 13, 2016. https://hbr.org/2016/07/the-data-driven-case-for-vacation

8. Heller, A.S., Shi, T.C., Ezie, C.E.C. et al. Association between real-world experiential diversity and positive affect relates to hippocampal–striatal functional connectivity. Nat Neurosci 23, 800–804 (2020). https://doi.org/10.1038/s41593-020-0636-4

ACKNOWLEDGEMENTS

Tremendous thanks goes to.....

Amy, for encouraging me to write the book and let go of perfectionism.

Debbie, Amy, and Mira for being willing to read, edit, and give me honest feedback about the book.

My clients, working with you fills me up and helps my development as much as it does yours.

My friends, Lelah, Mandy, Kathy, Joan, Heather, Regina, Amy, Chelsea, Debbie, Tommie Jean, Jacki, Becca, Veronique, Tracy, Kristen, Mary Beth, Kim, and many more that I haven't named. Thank you for your friendship, support, and love.

Fellow sports moms, thank you for the countless carpools, cheers for my kids, and sideline chats.

My kids, you make me laugh, fill me with delight, and I love being your mom.

Ted, for encouraging me, supporting me, believing in me, and especially seeing me.

My parents, for your endless support and watching my kids.

Thank you to everyone.

ABOUT THE AUTHOR

I am Alison Begor, a work-life balance coach who helps professional women create the time and space they want to finally have the work-life balance that they desire and deserve.

Not that long ago, I was juggling all the balls as a director at work and with two kids active in sports. I felt as if I were barely hanging on most days. I wasn't willing to give up my career and I knew I had to make changes to live a better life.

By creating strategies that worked for me I was able to create an additional five hours in my week for ME and I am now living the life I want on my terms.

My mission is to help women have fulfilling careers while also having time for family, fun and themselves.

I live in Kentucky with my two kids, my dog, and lots of sports equipment that can never be found when it's needed.